3 POINT
LANDING JOURNAL

Your powerful companion to go from just watching another video to actually taking action in your life.

BY: EVAN CARMICHAEL

ISBN: 978-1-7751263-2-4

Why Motivation Fades

You watch a video. You get motivated. 30 minutes later, that motivation is gone. Sound familiar? Do you want to fix it permanently?

Your motivation fades because you're living off the high of the energy of the person in the video instead of actually doing the work that's underneath their passion. Unless you want to play a video every 30 minutes to chase that high for the rest of your life, this journal is your powerful companion to give you sustained motivation as well as get results. Watching a video isn't results. Making meaningful changes in your life is results.

The 3 Point Landing Journal is broken down into two parts for each video. On the left side of each page you start by writing the name of the video and the date. Just doing this simple task you're already telling yourself that this is important . That watching this video is a commitment of your time and that's valuable. You're here to learn and get better, not just kill some time hoping to get motivated.

Underneath the date is an entire page for you to take notes. Watch the video, write down the rules that mean something to you. Record any quotes that stood out as memorable to you. Use the page to brainstorm how you can apply the information you've learned to your life. When you write things down, you're more likely to remember and you're more likely to do something about it. This is about taking action!

On the right side of each page is space for you to answer the 3 Point Landing Questions. At the end of most of my videos I ask 3 important questions. They are designed to make you stretch your comfort zone, challenge your status quo, and force you into action. Take a few minutes with each question. The answers, done correctly, will be life changing for you.

Doing this properly will likely mean that you can't watch as many videos from my channel. I'm good with that. You should be too. It's way better to watch one video, and make some significant progress in your life than watch 10 videos passively and never to anything. That's not how change happens.

This really comes down to the question of is your time valuable or not? You picking up this journal is a signal to yourself that it is. It's a new trigger for you environment that reminds you to value your time, respect yourself and your abilities, and build the life that you know you want to build.

I'm so excited for the journey you're about to go on! You get to learn from some of the brightest, most successful people on the planet and you're now armed with the tool to help you better digest their messages and apply them.

Share your progress with me. I'd love to hear about how you're growing, what you've learned, and the changes that you've made happen in your life as a result of using this journal.

Much love,

Evan Carmichael
#Believe

Video:

Date:

Notes:

Question 1:

Question 2:

Question 3:

Video:

Date:

Notes:

Question 1:

Question 2:

Question 3:

Video:

Date:

Notes:

Question 1:

Question 2:

Question 3:

Video:

Date:

Notes:

3 POINT LANDING JOURNAL

Question 1:

Question 2:

Question 3:

Video:

Date:

Notes:

Question 1:

Question 2:

Question 3:

Video:

Date:

Notes:

Question 1:

Question 2:

Question 3:

Video:

Date:

Notes:

Question 1:

Question 2:

Question 3:

Video:

Date:

Notes:

Question 1:

Question 2:

Question 3:

Video:

Date:

Notes:

Question 1:

Question 2:

Question 3:

Video:

Date:

Notes:

3 POINT LANDING JOURNAL

Question 1:

Question 2:

Question 3:

Video:

Date:

Notes:

Question 1:

Question 2:

Question 3:

Video:

Date:

Notes:

Question 1:

Question 2:

Question 3:

Video:

Date:

Notes:

Question 1:

Question 2:

Question 3:

Video:

Date:

Notes:

Question 1:

Question 2:

Question 3:

Video:

Date:

Notes:

Question 1:

Question 2:

Question 3:

Video:

Date:

Notes:

Question 1:

Question 2:

Question 3:

Video:

Date:

Notes:

Question 1:

Question 2:

Question 3:

Video:

Date:

Notes:

Question 1:

Question 2:

Question 3:

Video:

Date:

Notes:

3 POINT LANDING JOURNAL

Question 1:

Question 2:

Question 3:

Video:

Date:

Notes:

Question 1:

Question 2:

Question 3:

Video:

Date:

Notes:

Question 1:

Question 2:

Question 3:

Video:

Date:

Notes:

Question 1:

Question 2:

Question 3:

Video:

Date:

Notes:

Question 1:

Question 2:

Question 3:

Video:

Date:

Notes:

Question 1:

Question 2:

Question 3:

Video:

Date:

Notes:

Question 1:

Question 2:

Question 3:

Video:

Date:

Notes:

Question 1:

Question 2:

Question 3:

Video:

Date:

Notes:

Question 1:

Question 2:

Question 3:

Video:

Date:

Notes:

Question 1:

Question 2:

Question 3:

Video:

Date:

Notes:

Question 1:

Question 2:

Question 3:

Video:

Date:

Notes:

Question 1:

Question 2:

Question 3:

Video:

Date:

Notes:

Question 1:

Question 2:

Question 3:

Video:

Date:

Notes:

Question 1:

Question 2:

Question 3:

Video:

Date:

Notes:

Question 1:

Question 2:

Question 3:

Video:

Date:

Notes:

Question 1:

Question 2:

Question 3:

Video:

Date:

Notes:

3 POINT LANDING JOURNAL

Question 1:

Question 2:

Question 3:

Video:

Date:

Notes:

Question 1:

Question 2:

Question 3:

Video:

Date:

Notes:

Question 1:

Question 2:

Question 3:

✈ Video:

Date:

Notes:

Question 1:

Question 2:

Question 3:

Video:

Date:

Notes:

Question 1:

Question 2:

Question 3:

Video: ....

Date:

Notes:

Question 1:

Question 2:

Question 3:

Video:

Date:

Notes:

Question 1:

Question 2:

Question 3:

Video:

Date:

Notes:

3 POINT LANDING JOURNAL

Question 1:

Question 2:

Question 3:

Video:

Date:

Notes:

3 POINT LANDING JOURNAL

Question 1:

Question 2:

Question 3:

Video:

Date:

Notes:

Question 1:

Question 2:

Question 3:

Video:

Date:

Notes:

Question 1:

Question 2:

Question 3:

Video:

Date:

Notes:

3 POINT LANDING JOURNAL

Question 1:

Question 2:

Question 3:

Video:

Date:

Notes:

Question 1:

Question 2:

Question 3:

Video:

Date:

Notes:

Question 1:

Question 2:

Question 3:

Video: ....

Date:

Notes:

Question 1:

Question 2:

Question 3:

Video:
Date:
Notes:

3 POINT LANDING JOURNAL

Question 1:

Question 2:

Question 3:

Video:

Date:

Notes:

3 POINT LANDING JOURNAL

Question 1:

Question 2:

Question 3:

Video:

Date:

Notes:

3 POINT LANDING JOURNAL

Question 1:

Question 2:

Question 3:

Video:

Date:

Notes:

Question 1:

Question 2:

Question 3:

Video:

Date:

Notes:

3 POINT LANDING JOURNAL

Question 1:

Question 2:

Question 3:

Video:

Date:

Notes:

Question 1:

Question 2:

Question 3:

Video:

Date:

Notes:

Question 1:

Question 2:

Question 3:

Video: ....

Date:

Notes:

Question 1:

Question 2:

Question 3:

Video:

Date:

Notes:

Question 1:

Question 2:

Question 3:

Video:

Date:

Notes:

Question 1:

Question 2:

Question 3:

Video: ....

Date:

Notes:

3 POINT LANDING JOURNAL

Question 1:

Question 2:

Question 3:

Video:

Date:

Notes:

Question 1:

Question 2:

Question 3:

Video:

Date:

Notes:

3 POINT LANDING JOURNAL

Question 1:

Question 2:

Question 3:

Video:

Date:

Notes:

Question 1:

Question 2:

Question 3:

Video: ....

Date:

Notes:

Question 1:

Question 2:

Question 3:

Video:

Date:

Notes:

Question 1:

Question 2:

Question 3:

✈ Video: ....

Date:

Notes:

Question 1:

Question 2:

Question 3:

Video:

Date:

Notes:

Question 1:

Question 2:

Question 3:

Video:

Date:

Notes:

3 POINT LANDING JOURNAL

Question 1:

Question 2:

Question 3:

Video:

Date:

Notes:

3 POINT LANDING JOURNAL

Question 1:

Question 2:

Question 3:

Video:

Date:

Notes:

Question 1:

Question 2:

Question 3:

Video: ....

Date:

Notes:

Question 1:

Question 2:

Question 3:

Video:

Date:

Notes:

Question 1:

Question 2:

Question 3:

Video:

Date:

Notes:

Question 1:

Question 2:

Question 3:

Video:

Date:

Notes:

Question 1:

Question 2:

Question 3:

Video: ....

Date:

Notes:

Question 1:

Question 2:

Question 3:

Video:

Date:

Notes:

Question 1:

Question 2:

Question 3:

Video:

Date:

Notes:

Question 1:

Question 2:

Question 3:

Video:

Date:

Notes:

Question 1:

Question 2:

Question 3:

Video:

Date:

Notes:

Question 1:

Question 2:

Question 3:

✈ Video: _____

Date:

Notes:

3 POINT LANDING JOURNAL

Question 1:

Question 2:

Question 3:

Video:

Date:

Notes:

Question 1:

Question 2:

Question 3:

✈ Video: ⎯⎯⎯⎯⎯⎯⎯⎯⎯⎯⎯⎯⎯⎯⎯⎯

Date:

Notes:

3 POINT LANDING JOURNAL

Question 1:

Question 2:

Question 3:

Video:

Date:

Notes:

Question 1:

Question 2:

Question 3:

Video:

Date:

Notes:

Question 1:

Question 2:

Question 3:

Video:

Date:

Notes:

Question 1:

Question 2:

Question 3:

Video:

Date:

Notes:

Question 1:

Question 2:

Question 3:

Video:

Date:

Notes:

Question 1:

Question 2:

Question 3:

✈ Video: ....

Date:

Notes:

3 POINT LANDING JOURNAL

Question 1:

Question 2:

Question 3:

Video:
Date:
Notes:

3 POINT LANDING JOURNAL

Question 1:

Question 2:

Question 3:

Video: ....

Date:

Notes:

3 POINT LANDING JOURNAL

Question 1:

Question 2:

Question 3:

Video:

Date:

Notes:

Question 1:

Question 2:

Question 3:

Video:

Date:

Notes:

Question 1:

Question 2:

Question 3:

Video:

Date:

Notes:

3 POINT LANDING JOURNAL

Question 1:

Question 2:

Question 3:

Video:

Date:

Notes:

Question 1:

Question 2:

Question 3:

Video: ....

Date:

Notes:

Question 1:

Question 2:

Question 3:

Video:

Date:

Notes:

Question 1:

Question 2:

Question 3:

What's Next?

Congratulations on reaching the end! Here's what's next:

1)   Read over the journal pages. Feel proud of yourself for committing to learning instead of just consuming. Remember the person you were when you first started this journey and how much has changed since then. Give yourself a high five!

2)   The learning doesn't end here. Pick up another 3 Point Landing Journal and let's start in on the next set of videos!

3)   I'd love to have your help in spreading the message. If you liked the journal please consider sharing it with your friends and online so that more people can learn the wisdom here that is essential but not taught in schools.

4)   If you got great value from this journal, consider buying a copy for a friend. Some people are making this journal a part of their customer service where all new customers get a copy of the journal as a thank you. If it made a meaningful difference for you, it'll make a meaningful difference for others and you'll be remembered as the person who introduced them to it.

5)   Most importantly of all, take action. Don't let this journal just sit on your shelf collecting dust. Do something. You don't get changes in your life or business by just reading. You get changes by taking action.

I can't wait to see and hear about your progress. You're going to change the world and I'm honored to play a tiny part in your journey.

Much love,

Evan.
#Believe

About the Author

Evan Carmichael #Believes in entrepreneurs. At nineteen, he built then sold a biotech software company. At twenty-two, he was a venture capitalist helping raise $500 thousand to $15 million. Evan was named one of the Top 100 Great Leadership Speakers for your Next Conference by Inc. Magazine and one of the Top 40 Social Marketing Talents by Forbes. He has been interviewed or featured as an entrepreneur expert in the New York Times, the Wall Street Journal, Forbes, Mashable, and elsewhere. He runs EvanCarmichael.com, a popular YouTube channel for entrepreneurs, and his first book was Your One Word: The Powerful Secret to Creating a Business and Life That Matter. He speaks globally and is based in Toronto.

#Believe

Made in the USA
Columbia, SC
02 March 2021

33797291R00121